The Adventures of Ruby Pricklebottom
Book One: Ruby Has PKU

Copyright © 2016 by Brandon Parker

ISBN: 978-1532878787

Thanks to our corporate sponsor

with special thanks to the worldwide PKU community for their support

In no particular order...

Annaliese Martin, Marvin Family, Paden Family, Logan V. Yvette Irby, Gina M. Daunt, Lucas M., Gregor Hammerschmidt, Kendall Gray Flannery, The Sanfords, The Main Family, The Thoopsamoot's, Lucas's Grandma, The Clarks, Sue Mahar, Tammy Butler, Shane Garland, Kendall Flannery, The Burke Family, Deena C., In support of Owen Maxfield, The Forberg's, The Ryan Family, Elnaz, Lucy Wheelock, The Eaker Family, Dorothe, National PKU News, The Gourley Family, Vowell Family, The Pulvermacher Family, The Court Family, Liam Martens, Drew Croney, K. Thomassen, Aaron Burney, Matt & Kylie James, The Alaniz Family, James Family, Dampier Family, Isaac Heilers, Sawyer Layne Richards, Mary Jane Ryan, The family of Elliot Meyer, Hans & Lauren Huberland, Elin Thomassen & Tróndur G. Joensen, Julie Miller Everett and Family, Sophie & Lisa, Kiger Family, The Marcys, The Parker Family and the Lavender Family.

and thanks to all unlisted supporters as well.

For Maylee and all the other awesome kids with PKU.
Remember - you can do this and you are extraordinary!

The Adventures of Ruby Pricklebottom

Book One: Ruby Has PKU

by Anna and Brandon Parker

ilustrated by Steven Bybyk and Natalie Khmelovska

The Pricklebottom family had just settled in at home with their new baby when the phone rang.

"Hello?" answered Mr. Pricklebottom.

"Hello? Mr. Pricklebottom? It's about Baby Ruby.
We need you to come in to our office as soon as possible," replied a voice on the phone.

The next morning, the nervous hedgehog family listened as Dr. Bandit broke the news.

"Ruby has Phenylketonuria," said Dr. Bandit.

"Phenyl-what?" asked Mrs. Pricklebottom, holding Ruby a little closer.

"Phenylketonuria," said Dr. Bandit. "We call it 'PKU' for short. Ruby's body can't break down one of the amino acids in protein, so she will need a special diet."

The Pricklebottoms listened carefully as Dr. Bandit explained.

"This is protein. It is made up of 20 parts called amino acids. This one is called Phenylalanine, or 'phe'," he said, pointing to a chart on the wall.

"Ruby's body doesn't need very much phe, and eating too much of it can harm her body and brain."

Dr. Bandit continued, "Ruby should only eat as much phe as her body can use. That way, she can grow up to be a happy, healthy hedgehog."

Mr. Pricklebottom thought for a moment.

"How will we know how much phe her body can use?"
"You can check with a simple blood spot", answered Dr. Bandit. "Miss Babb will be Ruby's dietitian.
She will be waiting for you at the metabolic clinic and will show you exactly what to do. Everything is going to be just fine, you'll see."

Later, the Pricklebottoms arrived at the metabolic clinic, still feeling a bit confused and overwhelmed.

"Hello! I'm Miss Babb and I'll be taking good care of you and Ruby. It's so lovely to meet you! What a beautiful new daughter you have!" Miss Babb said warmly.

Mrs. Pricklebottom looked down at Ruby and asked, "Will she be okay?"

"Oh yes!" replied Miss Babb, "PKU isn't so bad! It's easily taken care of by putting Ruby on a low phe diet and medical formula. You'll count how much phe Ruby eats each day, and try to have her eat a 'magic number' of phe so that her body gets just exactly what it needs."

Miss Babb paused to make sure the new parents were understanding, then continued,

"Her magic number will change as she grows, so we like to get blood spots regularly to make sure she is on track."

"B-b-b-blood spots?!" Ruby's big brother asked. "What's that?"

"Oh, don't worry, Roscoe," Miss Babb answered. "Blood spots are just a little drop of Ruby's blood on special paper. We send it to the lab and the result is a number that tells us if there's too much, too little, or just enough phe in Ruby's diet."

Miss Babb smiled, then continued,

"You know Roscoe, Ruby is very lucky to have a big brother like you to watch out for her."

"Thanks!" Roscoe beamed.

The Pricklebottoms spent a little more time talking with Miss Babb and going over information about treating Ruby's PKU. Upon leaving the metabolic clinic, they were ready to get started with Ruby's special diet.

Time passed and Ruby grew more and more each day. Her family learned how to measure and count phe, and even Roscoe helped out. Ruby loved her formula, and life was good.

Miss Babb knew from the start that the Pricklebottoms would do a great job with Ruby's PKU, and she was right. She checked in with them regularly to let them know how Ruby's blood spot results came back. From time to time, Ruby's magic number needed to change a bit, just as they expected.

"Now remember, make sure Ruby drinks all of her formula and gets her magic number of phe each day," said Miss Babb. "Do her blood spot on Tuesday and we'll talk about the result as soon as it comes back from the lab."

"Thanks, Miss Babb! We'll talk soon,"
Mr. Pricklebottom replied.

That Tuesday afternoon, as Mrs. Pricklebottom was preparing to do the blood spot, she noticed that Ruby was nowhere to be seen.

"Roscoe, can you go find Ruby, please? It's time for her blood spot", said Mrs. Pricklebottom.

"Sure, mom!" Roscoe replied.

"Ruby? Ruuuby!" Roscoe called.

He heard a small sniffle coming from under Ruby's bed. Pulling up the blanket, he asked, "Ruby? What are you doing under there?"

"I hide, Roscoe," Ruby answered, tearfully.

Roscoe crawled under the bed to cuddle his sister.

"Why are you hiding?"

"Spot hurt. No ouchie," she answered.

"Ohhh," Roscoe said softly, "You don't want to do your blood spot?"

"No ouchie. No ouchie!" Ruby whined.

"Listen, Ruby. I know that doing your blood spot hurts a little. But it's over really fast, and it's really important," explained Roscoe.

He continued, "It tells us if your magic number of phe is still right for your body. Come on out, okay? I can hold your hand the whole time."

Ruby slowly came out from under the bed. Roscoe gave her a hug and they walked to the kitchen, where Mrs. Pricklebottom was waiting.

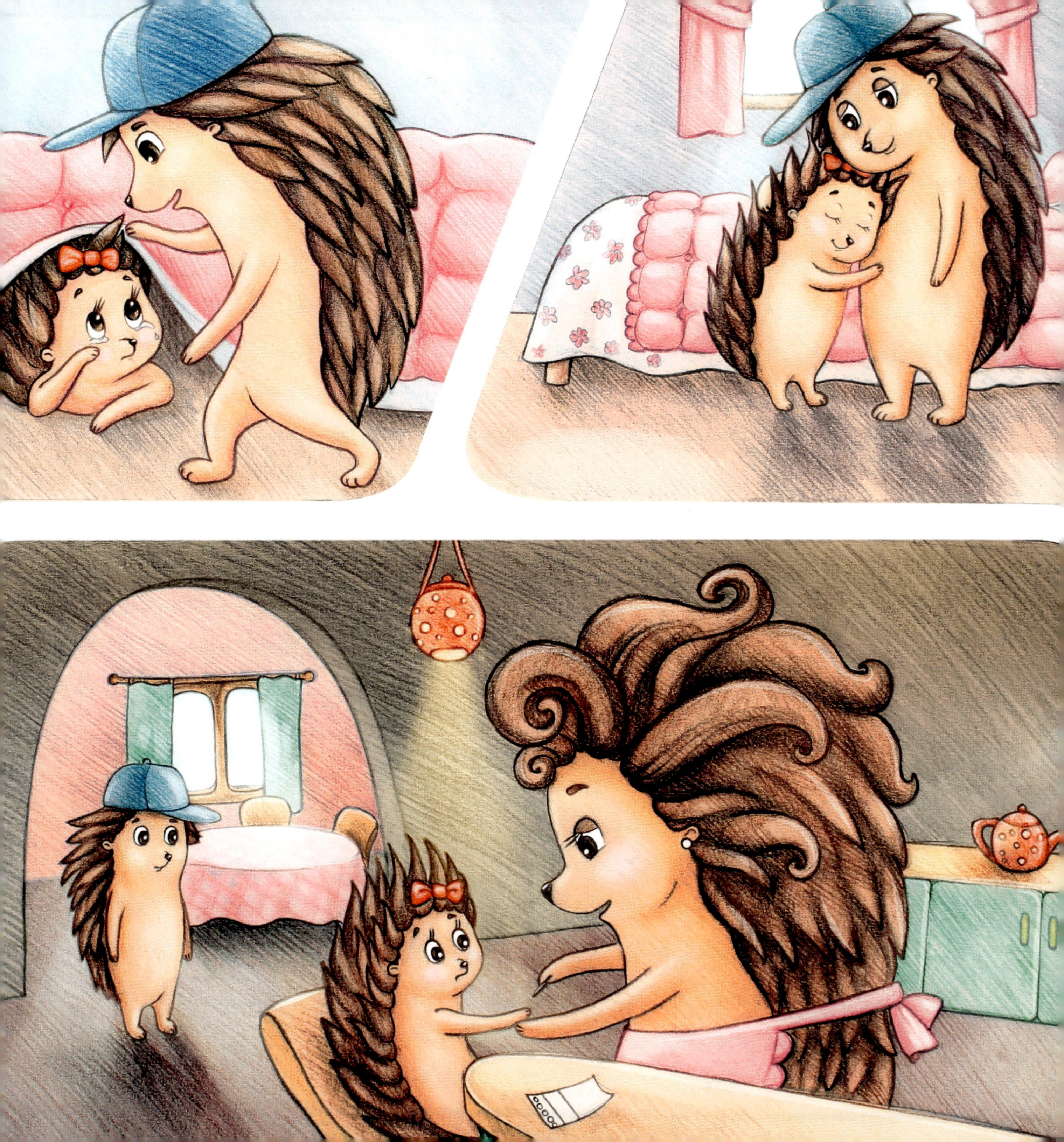

"One, two, three!"

Mrs. Pricklebottom pricked Ruby's finger on "three" and let a small drop of blood fall onto the paper. Ruby didn't even cry!

Roscoe wrapped a bandage around her finger and said, "Way to go, Ruby! Ready to go play?"

"Go! Go! Go!" she squealed and raced off down the hall, laughing as she went.

Roscoe chased after her, proud of how brave she had been.

Ruby had grown and grown. She was brave every time she had to do a blood spot and even picked out her own bandage. Before long, it was time for Ruby's first day of school.

The stump house was brewing with excitement as Mrs. Pricklebottom hurried to pack Ruby's lunch.

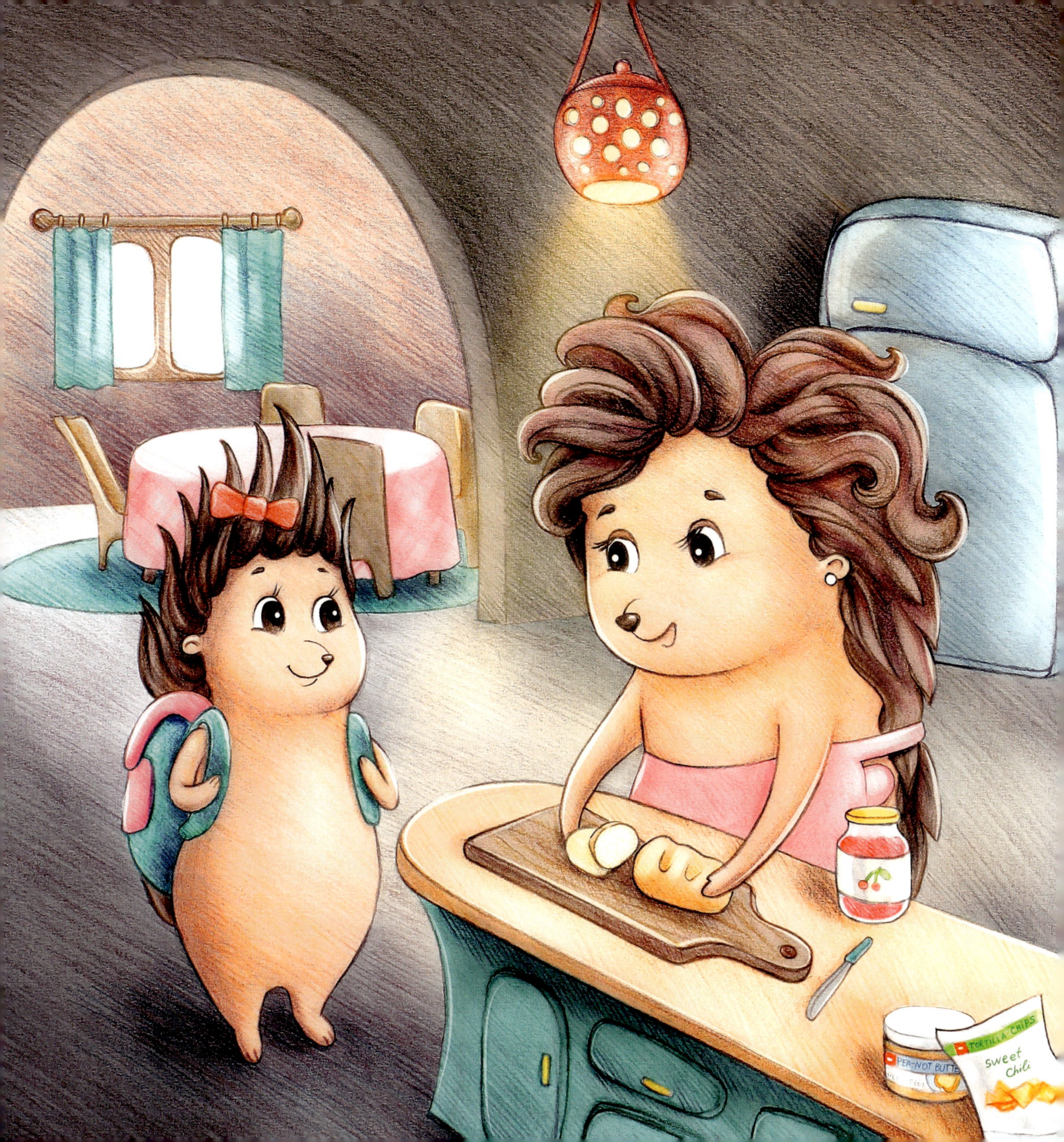
PEA-NOT BUTTE
TORTILLA CHIPS
Sweet Chili

Once Ruby was all set, she stood nervously with Roscoe as they waited on the bus.

"Don't worry, Ruby. You'll LOVE school! There are lots of fun things to do, and you'll make friends in no time. And if you need me, I'll be right down the hall," he assured her.

Ruby took a deep breath, smiled, and squeezed Roscoe's hand.

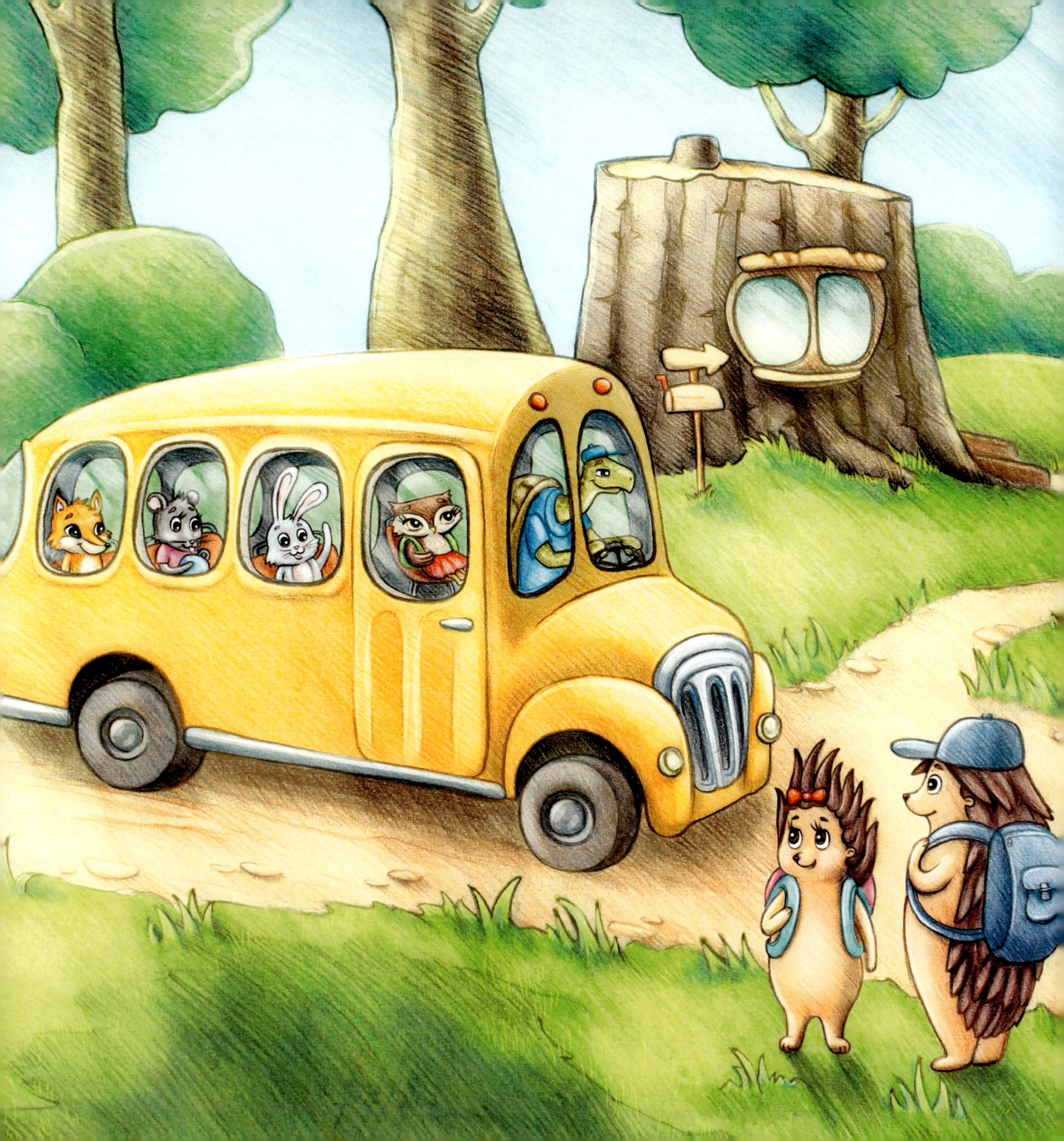

As they walked into the school, Roscoe gave Ruby one more bit of advice.

"Remember Ruby, don't share snacks with anyone. You have to stick to your diet," he said. "You know what your body needs. Stick to your magic number!"

"Got it!" replied Ruby, as she gave Roscoe one last hug.

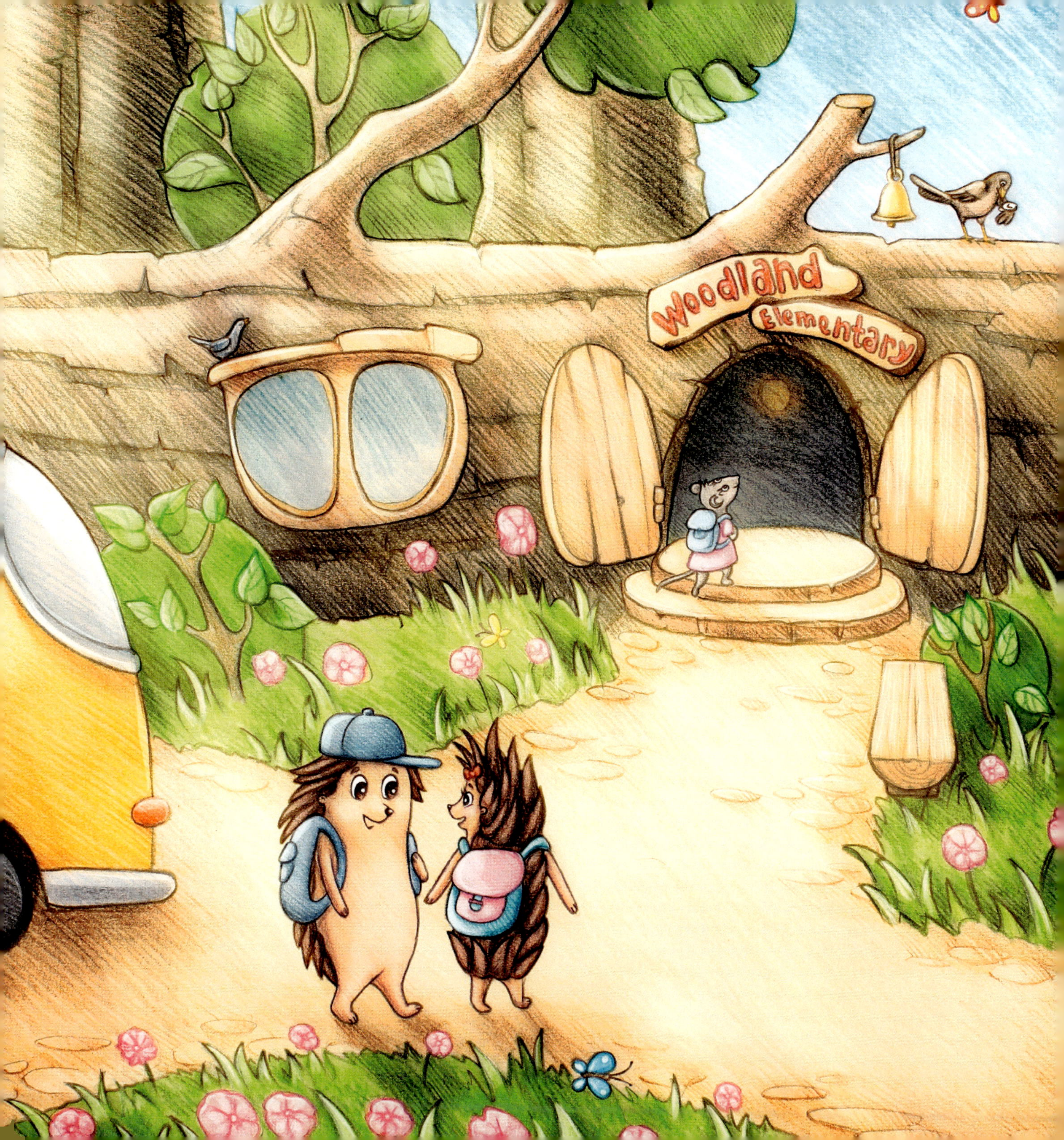
Woodland
Elementary

"You must be Ruby", said Miss Jay, "Come on in. We're going to have a great day! I've heard all about you. Did you know I was Roscoe's teacher, too?"

Ruby nodded.

"We're having some play time. Why don't you find your desk and put your things away? Then, you may choose an activity."

ABCDEFG

Ruby came in cautiously and found her desk.
A small, grey mouse scampered over to her.

"Hi, I'm Molly. Want to play blocks with me?"

Ruby smiled and felt relieved to have already made a friend.

"Hi, I'm Ruby. Sure, let's go!"

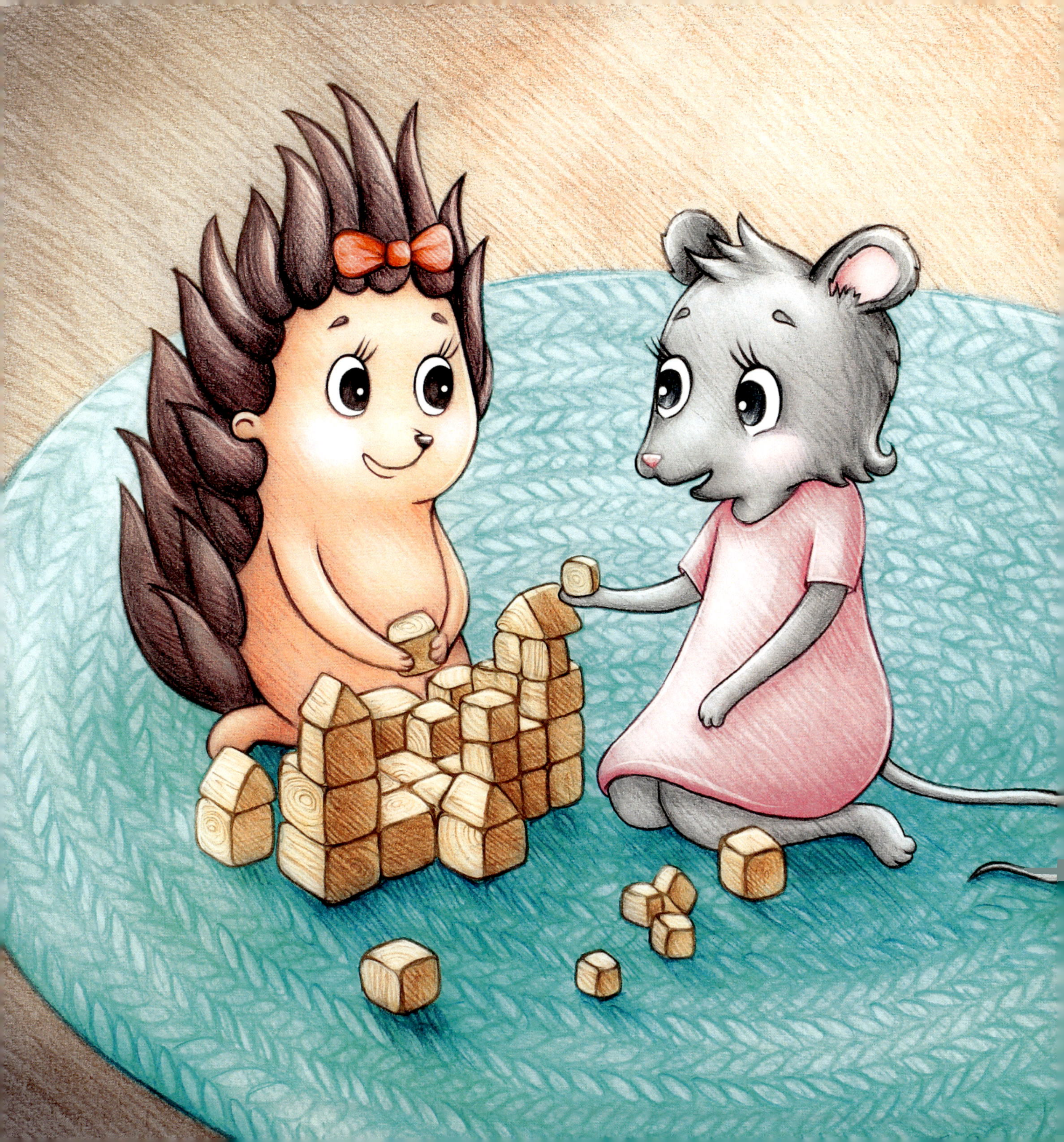

Molly and Ruby played all morning, and Miss Jay even let them sit by one another at lunch.

"Hey Ruby," Molly said. "Do you want a piece of my mom's special cheese? She makes the BEST cheese wheels!"

Ruby replied, "I'd better not...but thanks anyway. I have PKU, so I only eat my special foods and drink a special formula." Molly looked puzzled.

"Well, can't you have just a little nibble?" she asked.

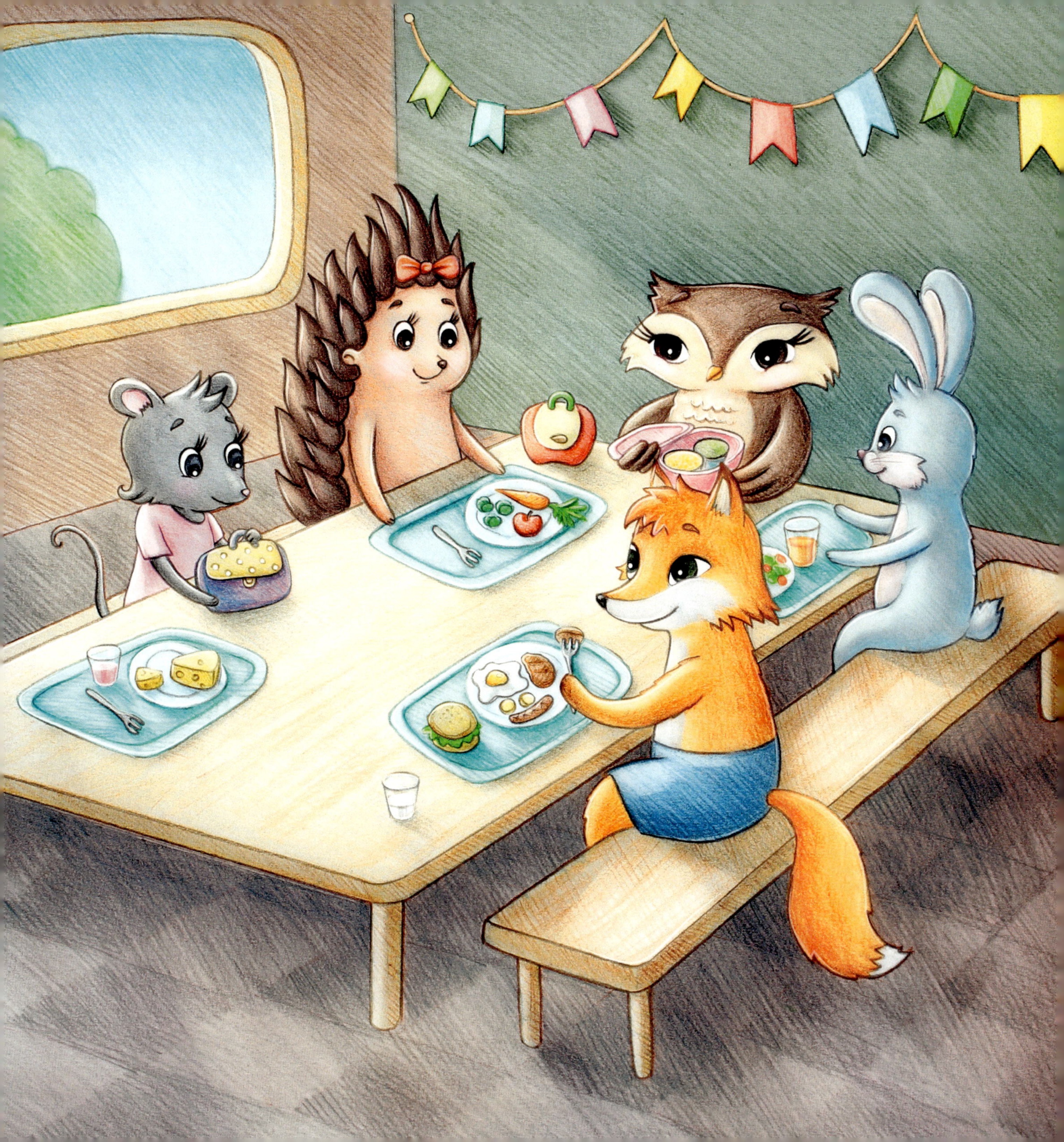

"PKU is sort of serious, Molly." Ruby continued, "If I eat things I'm not supposed to have, I will feel yucky and my body won't be healthy any more. It can even hurt my brain! It's nice that you want to share, but I know that my special low protein foods keep me feeling my best. Okay?"

Molly nodded, finally understanding.

"Sure, Ruby. I want you to be okay! Wow, I'm glad you know so much about your PKU!"

The two friends finished eating their lunches and chattered happily. Ruby told Molly all about her blood spots and her magic phe number, and Molly told Ruby how brave she thought Ruby must be to handle her PKU so well.

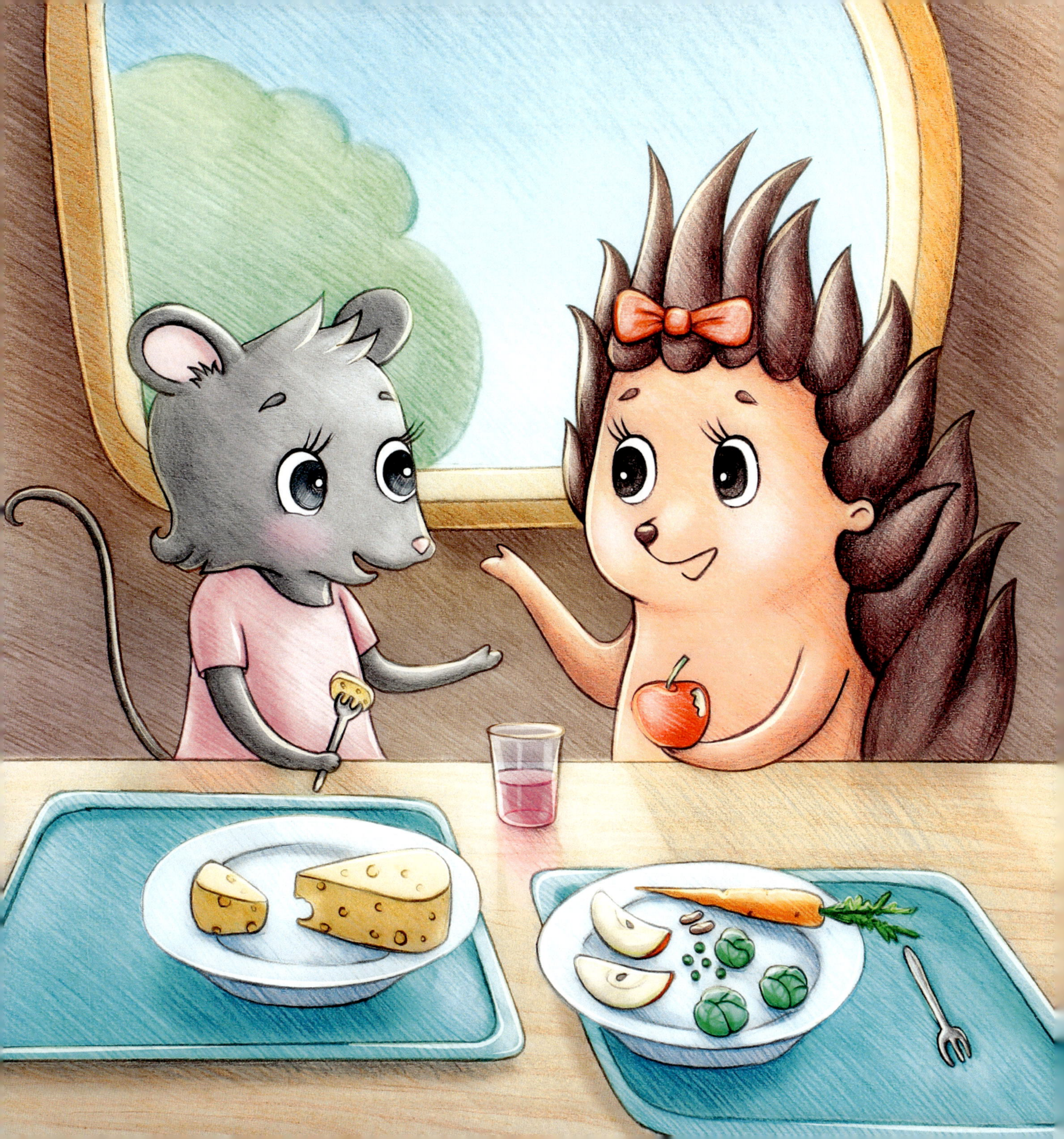

As Roscoe and Ruby rode the bus back home that afternoon, they talked about the day. Roscoe had just finished telling Ruby about his new teacher when he spotted a box at their front door.

"Look, Ruby!" he exclaimed. "Your new PKU food arrived!"

Ruby skipped off the bus, excited to see her yummy new goodies. Getting her food in the mail was almost like opening a present! It was a great surprise and a perfect ending to her day.

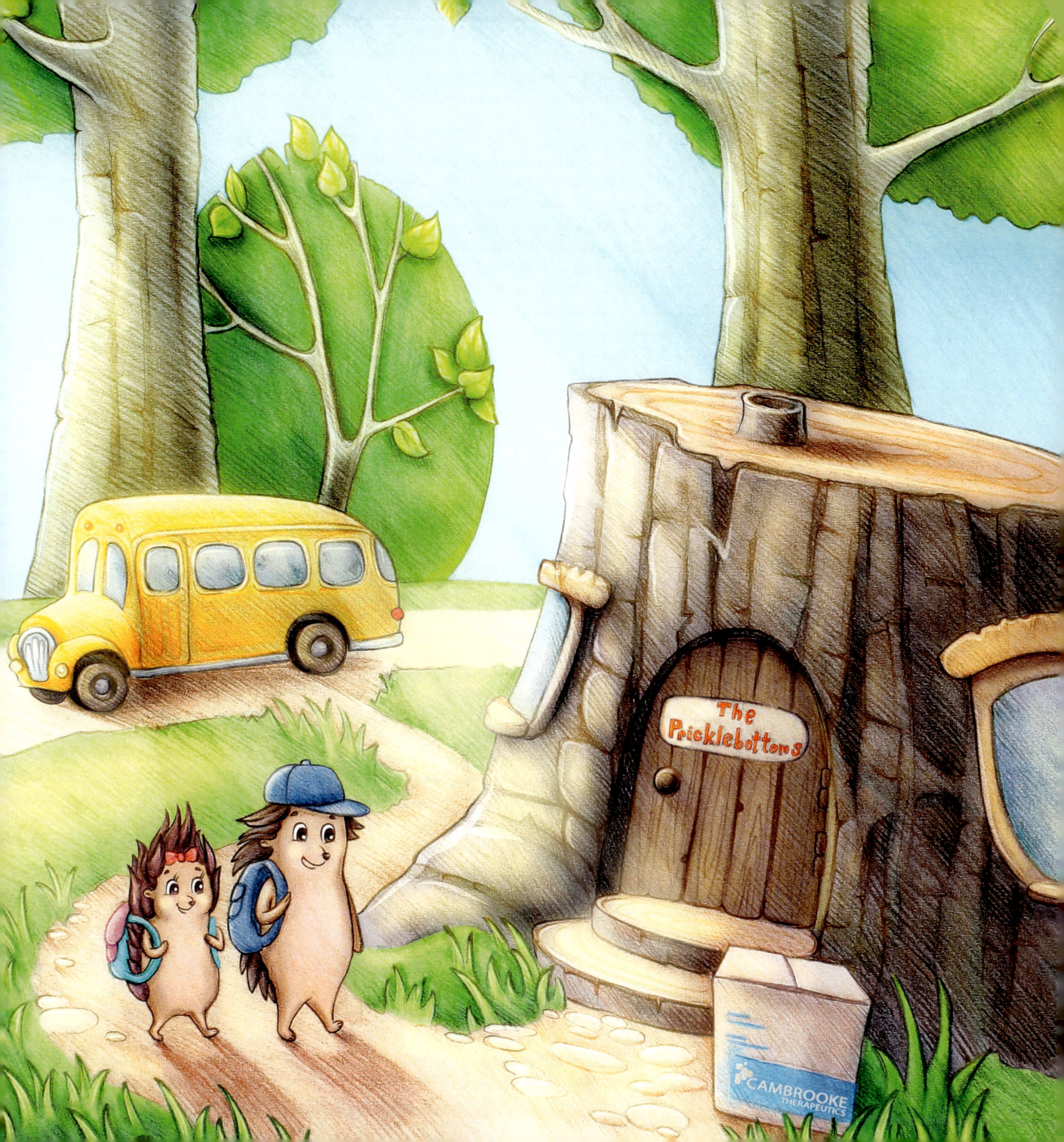
The
Pricklebottoms
CAMBROOKE
THERAPEUTICS

That night, at dinner, Ruby had a brand new low protein dish. The Pricklebottoms listened as Ruby told them about Molly and how she had taught her all about PKU. She had been brave and strong. It was in that moment that Mr. and Mrs. Pricklebottom knew that Ruby would be even more than okay.

Ruby Pricklebottom would be extraordinary!

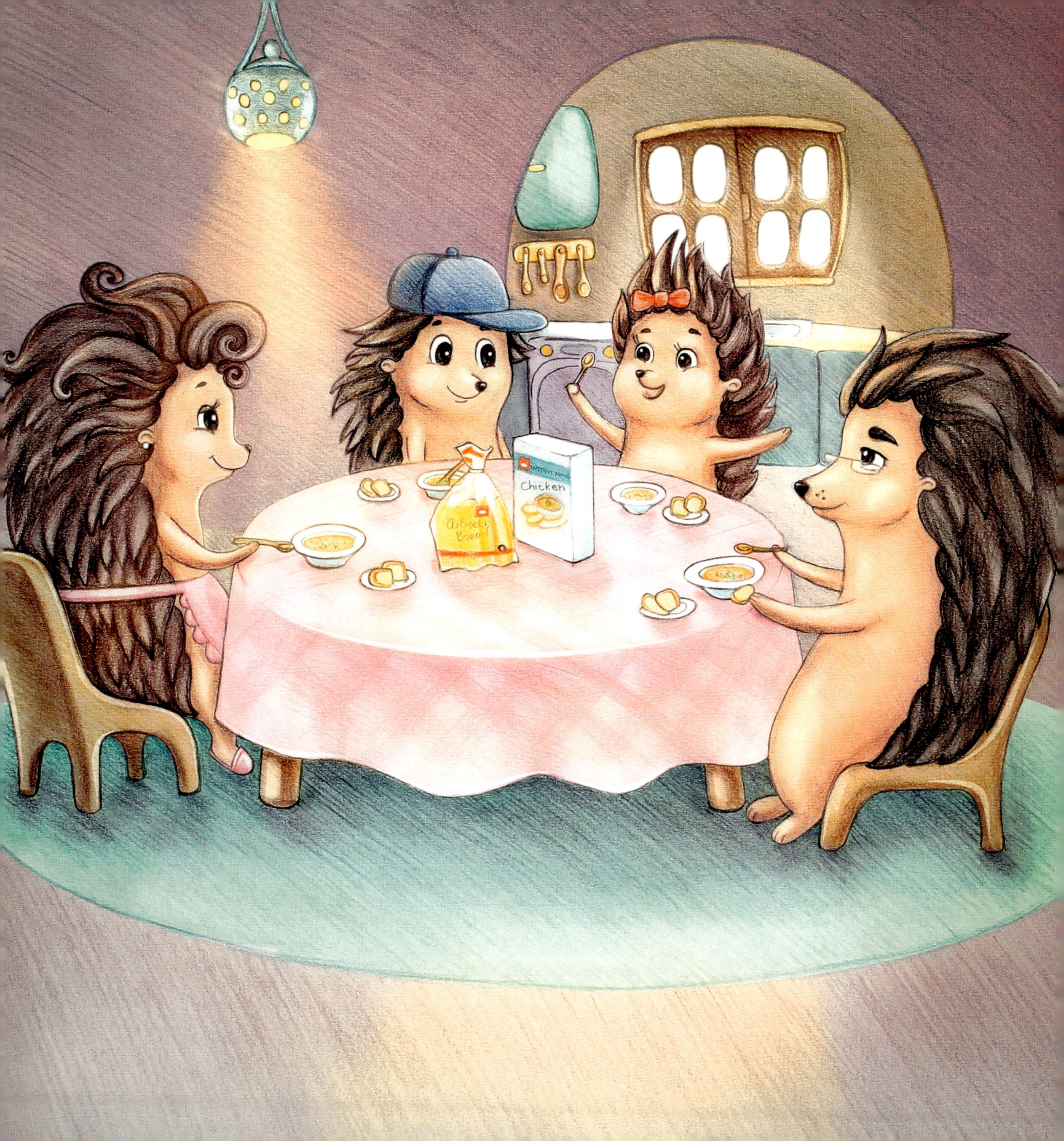
Chicken

About the Authors

Anna Parker got her master's degree in Elementary Education in 2010 and is currently a second grade teacher in Ringgold, Georgia. She is no stranger to the PKU world, having been successfully on diet for her entire life. Anna was diagnosed with classical PKU at the Emory Metabolic Clinic in Atlanta, Georgia, in 1982, and is active in the PKU community both in Georgia and on a national level. She has been a friend, mentor, speaker, advocate, and role model for others with PKU, and feels strongly that PKU does not define her. Her motto regarding PKU is "people will remember you for what you did and how you made them feel, not what was on your plate."

Brandon Parker studied Business Administration at Bryan College. He utilized his resourcefulness, design experience, and creativity to produce Ruby Pricklebottom. Brandon's first introduction to PKU began after meeting Anna. He quickly learned the ins and outs of the diet, and swept Anna off her feet by whipping up low protein meals for her on a regular basis.

Brandon and Anna married in 2006 and had their first daughter, Emory, in 2011. Emory was named in honor of the doctors and dietitians from the Emory Metabolic Clinic that had such a huge impact on Anna's life. In early 2012, Brandon and Anna became aware of a little girl with PKU from China, in need of adoption. With much prayer, fundraising, and hard work, Brandon and Anna were able to adopt and bring Maylee home in winter of 2014.
The Parkers are thankful for the journeys that PKU has taken them on over the years, and look forward to what God has in store for them next!

This book is proudly sponsored by

CAMBROOKE THERAPEUTICS

Cambrooke is proud to sponsor the Adventures of Ruby Pricklebottom -- a much needed educational story to teach families and children about phenylketonuria (PKU). PKU was the first genetic disease screened at birth and is managed almost entirely with nutritional therapy. "Ruby" helps families understand how to cope with and manage growing up with this lifelong dietary restriction.

Cambrooke Therapeutics was founded in 2000 by David & Lynn Paolella-- parents of two children diagnosed at birth with PKU. Cambrooke was created to provide a "complete dietary therapy" for PKU patients. The company develops and manufactures special foods and protein supplements to serve many inborn errors of protein metabolism (IEPM) - collectively known as "Medical Foods". Today, Cambrooke has more than one hundred medical food products.

Following eight years of NIH funded University research, Cambrooke's Glytactin® protein is the world's first PKU protein formula (substitute) to include a natural whole protein source derived from dairy whey. Clinical studies have shown this protein source is often better tolerated and preferred by patients and clinicians.

Cambrooke Therapeutics continues to expand its collaboration with academic research and is growing as a global innovator in medical nutrition. Its Boston based development and manufacturing team are providing best of class medical therapy for patients on 4 continents.

In the United States, access to care is not guaranteed for all IEPM patients. The CAMBROOKEcare ™ Team is dedicated to helping patients obtain essential insurance reimbursement for their long term care. CAMBROOKEcare ™ offers a full service program designed for one very important thing: access to life-saving medical food while minimizing financial hardship.

For more information on Cambrooke and ordering products visit: www.Cambrooke.com or call 1-866-456-9776.
Save 15% on your total Cambrooke Low Protein Food order.
Use or mention code RUBY16. One time use per customer.

Thank you to the PKU community for your support of this book and especially the Kickstarter pledgers!

CAMBROOKE
THERAPEUTICS

Made in the USA
Monee, IL
28 March 2020